Jackie Robinson

CORNERSTONES OF FREEDOM™

SECOND SERIES

Dan Elish

Children's Press®
A Division of Scholastic Inc.
New York • Toronto • London • Auckland • Sydney
Mexico City • New Delhi • Hong Kong
Danbury, Connecticut

Photographs © 2005: AP/Wide World Photos: 7, 13, 14, 15, 17, 21, 22, 24, 25, 33, 38; Corbis Images/Bettmann: bottom cover (Herb Scharfman), top cover, 3, 4, 8, 9, 11, 18, 20, 26, 28, 29, 30, 32, 34, 36, 37, 39, 40, 45; Getty Images/Hulton Archive: 5, 6, 12, 27, 44; Negro Leagues Baseaball Museum, Inc.: 16.

Library of Congress Cataloging-in-Publication Data
Elish, Dan.
 Jackie Robinson / Dan Elish.
   p. cm. — (Cornerstones of freedom. Second series)
 Includes bibliographical references and index.
 ISBN 0-516-23635-0
 1. Robinson, Jackie, 1919–1972—Juvenile literature. 2. Baseball players—United States—Biography—Juvenile literature. I. Title. II. Series.
 GV865.R6E45 2005
 796.357'092—dc22   2004017704

1 2 3 4 5 6 7 8 9 10 R 14 13 12 11 10 09 08 07 06 05

JULY 23, 1962, WAS AN EXCITING day for baseball fans across America. Their attention was focused on Cooperstown, New York. It was there that Jackie Robinson, second baseman for the Brooklyn Dodgers, was to be **inducted** into the Baseball Hall of Fame.

FIELDING MARK FOR SECOND BASEMAN
PLAYING IN 150 OR MORE GAMES WITH .992.
LEAD N.L. IN STOLEN BASES IN 1947 AND
1949. MOST VALUABLE PLAYER IN 1949.
LIFETIME BATTING AVERAGE .311. JOINT
RECORD HOLDER FOR MOST DOUBLE PLAYS
BY SECOND BASEMAN 137 IN 1951.
LED SECOND BASEMEN IN DOUBLE
PLAYS 1949-50-51-52.

Jackie Robinson played for the Brooklyn Dodgers, wearing jersey number 42.

Jack "Jackie" Roosevelt Robinson was one of the best ballplayers of his time. His performance on the field was impressive. But Jackie was respected even more for the strength of his character.

In 1947, he became the first African American to play in the Major Leagues. At that time, American society was very much divided between races. Many white Americans couldn't stand the idea of a black man playing in the Major Leagues. Jackie was called horrible names. He even received death threats. To his credit, Jackie always behaved with great

dignity. His actions helped pave the way for black athletes after him. Sportswriter Roger Kahn put it this way, "Jackie Robinson made his country and you and me and all of us a shade more free."

GROWING UP POOR

Jackie Robinson was born in Cairo, Georgia, on January 31, 1919. His grandfather was born into slavery. His father, Jerry Robinson, worked on a farm for twelve dollars a month. His mother, Mallie, worked as a maid.

Six months after Jackie was born, his father took a trip to Texas. He never returned. Mallie had to work very hard to support Jackie and his four siblings, Edgar, Frank, Mack, and Willa Mae. Looking for a fresh start, Mallie decided to move her family West.

After a long trip cross-country by train, Jackie and his family settled in Pasadena, California. Mallie worked long hours cleaning homes. She was finally able to scrape together enough money to buy a small house in a white

Young Jackie Robinson did not have an easy childhood. His father left his family when he was a baby. Though his mother worked hard to support the family, they were very poor.

Jackie Robinson (second from left), his mother, and siblings posed for this family portrait in 1925.

neighborhood. Still, the family was very poor. As Jackie remembered, "Some days we wouldn't have eaten at all if it hadn't been for the leftovers my mother was able to bring home from her job."

With his mother at work, someone had to look after baby Jackie. This job fell to his sister, Willa Mae. While Willa Mae was in kindergarten, Jackie played in the sandbox in the school playground. Willa Mae would keep an eye on him through the window, then run out at lunchtime to spend time with him. Jackie was happy when he was old enough to attend school on his own.

Jackie's first experience with racism occurred when he was eight years old. One day a neighbor girl started calling him horrible names because he was black. Soon Jackie was in a stone-throwing fight with the girl's father. Finally the man's wife came out of the house and made her husband stop. Mallie was proud that Jackie had stood up for himself. This kind of **prejudice** would follow Jackie all the way to the Major Leagues.

Young Jackie Robinson plays catch with friends.

★ ★ ★ ★

Mack Robinson (left), Jackie's brother, competes at the 1936 Olympic Track and Field tryouts. Jesse Owens, in the Ohio jersey, went on to compete in and win four gold medals in the 1936 Olympics in Berlin.

A GREAT ATHLETE

Jackie loved sports when he was growing up. His classmates noticed that Jackie could do things that no one else could. In dodgeball, he would always be the last child standing. The games would have to stop because no one could hit him.

All the Robinson children were outstanding athletes. Edgar roller-skated and played softball. Frank and Mack were world-class sprinters. In the 1936 Olympics, Mack placed second to the famous American runner Jesse Owens in the 200-meter dash. Willa Mae was a top sprinter and also did well at basketball and soccer. Jackie's first love was track and field. But as his brother Mack put it, "He was great in all sports."

Still, when Jackie graduated from high school, no major university offered him a scholarship. In that era, big-time college sports were almost completely closed to African Americans. So Jackie chose to attend Pasadena Junior College because it was close to home. He played on the school's football team. In his first year as quarterback, he led the team to five straight victories. At the end of the season, it was discovered that he had played the games on a partially broken ankle!

Jackie Robinson wasn't just a great baseball player. He excelled at many sports and was a star quarterback on the Pasadena Junior College football team.

★ ★ ★ ★

Jackie graduated from Pasadena Junior College in 1940. He was offered several athletic scholarships. He chose the University of California at Los Angeles (UCLA). There he starred in basketball, football, track and field, and baseball. It seemed as though Jackie could do anything.

The color of Jackie's skin always held him back. If he had been white he would clearly have been offered a contract to play professional basketball, football, or baseball. Instead Jackie dropped out of UCLA so that he could find work to help support his mother. By that time Jackie had met a pretty nursing student named Rachel Isum. Though he and Rachel were falling in love, Jackie took a job as a construction worker in Hawaii.

Then on December 7, 1941, everything changed. In a surprise attack, Japanese planes dropped bombs on American battleships docked at Pearl Harbor, Hawaii. Suddenly the United States was knee-deep in World War II. In 1942, Jackie joined the Army.

IN THE ARMY

In the Army, Jackie continued to face racial prejudice. In May 1942, Jackie was shipped to Fort Riley, Kansas, for basic training. Blacks were allowed to fight in the Army, but all units were **segregated** by race.

TWO SPORTS, TWO CITIES

Jackie once played two sports in two cities on the same day! On May 8, 1938, Jackie took three long jumps at a morning track meet in Pomona, California. His final jump was 25 feet and 6 1/2 inches, breaking his older brother Mack's junior-college record. Jackie then drove to Glendale. He led his baseball team to a 5–3 victory. That year Jackie was voted the most valuable player in Southern California junior-college baseball.

The USS *Arizona* sinks in Pearl Harbor on December 7, 1941. After the Japanese attacked Pearl Harbor, the United States entered World War II.

In January 1943, Jackie became a second lieutenant. He was soon named an officer of his unit. It wasn't long before Jackie had to handle his first complaint. Several men told Jackie about the seating arrangement in the post exchange, where soldiers gathered for snacks and conversation. Only six or seven seats were set aside for blacks. As a result, many of Jackie's men were forced to stand while whites sat.

To address the problem, Jackie phoned a man named Major Hafner. Hafner was in charge of the seating. When

11

Jackie Robinson and another army recruit train with rifles. Robinson enlisted in the U.S. army in 1942.

Major Hafner said something insulting about African Americans, Jackie complained to his **superior** officer. Soon more seats were placed in the post exchange for blacks.

Jackie was later sent to Fort Hood, Texas. One day he got on a bus and sat near the front. The driver stopped and demanded that Jackie move to the back because he was black. Jackie refused.

When the bus arrived in Fort Hood, Jackie was questioned by military police. He was later brought up on charges of **insubordination.** This meant he had to face a court martial, or a military trial, to see if he could stay in the Army. Jackie was found innocent. He had stood up for his rights once again.

THE KANSAS CITY MONARCHS

In the early 1900s, blacks were not allowed to play professional baseball with whites. "Negro Leagues" had been formed in the late 1800s. Its teams were made up entirely of black players.

At the time he was leaving the Army in fall 1944, Jackie ran into a black man named Alexander. Alexander had once

JOE LOUIS

Joe Louis was the first black athlete accepted by white Americans. Born in 1914, Louis became one of the greatest boxers of all time. In 1938, on the eve of World War II, Louis defeated German boxer Max Schmeling. After the victory, Louis became a hero to the entire nation. His son, Joe Louis Jr., said that, "by winning, he became white America's first black hero."

Joe Louis became an American hero when he defeated German boxer Max Schmeling in 1938.

Jackie Robinson joined the Kansas City Monarchs baseball team in 1945. He played with the team for just one season.

Satchel Paige was elected to the Baseball Hall of Fame in 1971.

been a member of the Kansas City Monarchs, a baseball team in the Negro Leagues. He told Jackie that there was decent money to be made playing "black baseball." Needing a job, Jackie was interested. He wrote a letter to the Monarchs, who quickly invited him to spring training.

JOSH GIBSON AND SATCHEL PAIGE

Because of racial discrimination, some great black players, such as Josh Gibson, never got to play in the majors. They made little money, and their great talent went unseen by most white fans. Others, like Satchel Paige, were luckier and had a chance to play in the Major Leagues after Jackie Robinson broke the color barrier.

In the spring of 1945, Jackie joined the Monarchs. He quickly became one of the team's star players. At first, Jackie was thrilled to be paid to play baseball. But as time went on he grew more and more unhappy.

Jackie Robinson (front row, third from left) and teammates pose for a Kansas City Monarchs team picture in 1945.

Playing in the Negro Leagues, he wrote later, was "a pretty miserable way to make a buck." The travel schedules were exhausting. The Monarchs played in Kansas City, Missouri, and traveled by bus. One time the team left Kansas City on a Sunday night and arrived in Philadelphia, Pennsylvania, on Tuesday morning. That night they played a doubleheader, or two games in a row. They then got right back on the bus to head to their next game.

On top of the tiring travel schedule, it was nearly impossible to find places to eat. Most restaurants wouldn't serve blacks. As Jackie wrote, "You were lucky if they . . . permitted you to carry out some greasy hamburgers in a paper bag."

By late August 1945, Jackie was tired of the Negro Leagues. He decided to quit baseball and move back to Los Angeles. There he would marry Rachel and get a job coaching school sports.

BRANCH RICKEY

Jackie wasn't finished with baseball just yet, though. Unknown to Jackie, a Major League team called the Brooklyn Dodgers had quietly been looking for the right black ball player. The man behind the search was the team's general manager, Branch Rickey.

Rickey was a white man who was known for his brilliant baseball mind. He had been vice president and business manager of the St. Louis Cardinals for twenty-seven years. In that period, Rickey fought against a rule that said that black fans had to sit in a separate section of the St. Louis ballpark. Rickey's bosses maintained that white fans

Branch Rickey was born in Ohio in 1881. When he was in college he spent two seasons as a catcher in the American League. Best known for his accomplishments as a baseball executive, he was elected to the Baseball Hall of Fame in 1967.

Kenesaw Mountain Landis was a federal judge who became the first commissioner of baseball in 1920. He served until his death in 1944, and none of his decisions as commissioner was ever reversed.

wouldn't want to come to the games if they had to sit with blacks. As Rickey said later, "The utter **injustice** of it was always in my mind."

Meanwhile blacks were pushing to break into the Major Leagues. In December 1943, a famous black singer, Paul Robeson, met with baseball commissioner Judge Kenesaw Mountain Landis. Robeson argued that if blacks were good enough to die fighting in World War II, they were good enough to play baseball. Landis was against **integrating** baseball, but he was embarrassed by Robeson's words. He soon found himself saying that Major League teams were free to hire blacks if they chose.

Of course, Landis thought that no owner would want to sign a black player. Rickey proved him wrong. But he knew that the first African American player in the majors had to be special. This player had to be a star. He would have to excite the fans and help Brooklyn win ballgames. He also had to be able to stand up to terrible abuse and be a strong role model for blacks and whites across the nation.

Rickey knew that many Americans would be furious to see a black man in the Major Leagues. To keep his plans secret, he told people that he was looking for black ballplayers to form a new team called the Brooklyn Brown Dodgers. This team would play when the Brooklyn Dodgers were out of town.

Rickey's **scouts** circled the Negro Leagues. They were looking for a player who could run, throw, and hit with power. In the end, Jackie was given the best shot at succeeding. He was tough, well-spoken, and a great athlete.

On August 24, Jackie was warming up before one of his final games for the Monarchs. Suddenly he heard a white man yell his name from the sidelines. The man introduced

"IF ONLY THEY WERE WHITE"

In 1910, Branch Rickey was a coach for the Ohio Wesleyan College baseball team. During that time, a hotel once refused to give a room to a black player named Charley Thomas. Thomas began to cry. He told Rickey that if only his hands and skin were white he would "be as good as anybody then." Rickey said, "The day will come when they won't have to be white." Thirty-five years later Branch Rickey made his words come true by signing Jackie Robinson to a contract.

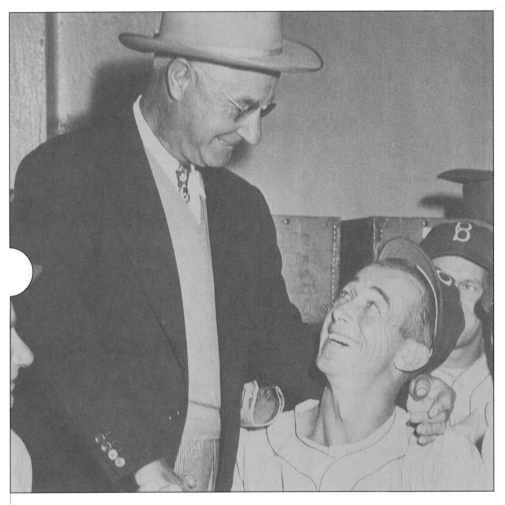

himself as Clyde Sukeforth. The name meant nothing to Jackie. But when Sukeforth said he worked for Branch Rickey and the Brooklyn Dodgers, Jackie was all ears. He then asked if Jackie would be willing to throw a few balls. He wanted to see how strong his arm was.

"Why is Mr. Rickey interested in my arm?" Jackie asked. "Why is he interested in me?"

Jackie was about to find out.

A FATEFUL MEETING

Sukeforth later brought Jackie to Branch Rickey's office in New York. Rickey's first question was "You got a girl?" Jackie told Rickey about his fiancée, Rachel. Rickey was pleased. He said, "When we get through today you may want to call her up because there are times when a man needs a woman by his side."

Then Rickey asked Jackie if he understood why he had been brought in for the meeting. Jackie replied that he thought it was about playing for the Brooklyn Brown Dodgers. Rickey said no. "I'm interested in you as a candidate for the Brooklyn National League club." As Jackie later wrote, "I was thrilled, scared, and excited. . . . Most of all, I was speechless."

Jackie Robinson and Branch Rickey have a conversation over dinner. Rickey had to be absolutely sure that Robinson could handle the pressure of being the first African American to play major league baseball.

Then Rickey said, "I know you're a good ballplayer. What I don't know is whether you have the guts." He went on: "We can win only if we can convince the world that I'm doing this because you're a great ballplayer and a fine gentleman."

Jackie could feel how much this meant to Rickey. But Rickey wasn't finished. He had to make absolutely sure that Jackie knew what he would be up against. He told Jackie that balls would be thrown at his head and that players would try to spike him with their cleats. Then he uttered some of the horrible names fans and players would call him.

Finally Rickey exclaimed, "Robinson, I'm looking for a ballplayer with guts enough not to fight back." Branch Rickey knew that many white fans would try to make Jackie so upset that he would start a fight in the ballpark. That

Jackie Robinson signs a contract with the Montreal Royals, the Dodger minor league team.

would prove to the country that a black man couldn't play in the majors.

Branch Rickey liked what he saw. He offered Jackie a contract for the Montreal Royals, the Dodger minor league team. If Jackie played well in Montreal, he would be promoted to the Brooklyn Dodgers.

LIFE AS A ROYAL

Word spread quickly that the Dodgers had signed Jackie. Many sportswriters and white players, however, didn't think he was good enough to play in the majors. The famous pitcher Bob Feller said, "He couldn't hit an inside pitch to save his neck. If he were a white man, I doubt if they would even consider him as big-league material."

The Montreal Royals met for spring training each February in Daytona Beach, Florida. Jackie and Rachel had to travel from Los Angeles. The long trip was anything but easy. When their crowded plane landed in New Orleans, Louisiana, to refuel, they were asked to get off. At first Jackie and Rachel didn't know why. They soon found out that, in the South, a black person could be bumped out of his seat for a white person if the plane was full. On top of that, no restaurant in the New Orleans airport would serve them.

Their problems still weren't over. The next day, Jackie and Rachel were bumped off yet another plane. In the end, they decided to travel the rest of the way by bus. But even that proved difficult. The driver made them sit in the back so that whites could sit up front.

Jackie Robinson played with the Montreal Royals during the 1946 season and had the best batting average in the International League.

Robinson fields a ball during infield practice. He quickly proved himself to be capable of major league play.

Once Jackie reached training camp, it didn't take long for him to prove himself on the field. His teammates were impressed by his speed and energy. Still, Jackie had to deal with near-constant prejudice. During one game, a policeman ordered him off the field. He claimed that blacks weren't allowed to play with whites.

Jackie quickly became the most talked-about minor-league ballplayer in history. Much of the talk was racist. Players from the other teams sometimes screamed curses from their dugouts. On the other hand, he also had many

★ ★ ★ ★

BATTING AVERAGES

If a player gets three hits for every ten times he is up to bat, his batting average is .300. Because hitting a baseball is one of the most difficult things to do in sports, any average over .300 is considered excellent.

fans. And Jackie produced on the ballfield. He finished the season with a .349 batting average. He stole forty bases and led the Royals to the minor-league championship.

Montreal's manager was Clay Hopper. Hopper was born in the South. In the beginning of the season, Hopper had begged Branch Rickey not to make him manage a black man. Rickey had replied, "You can manage correctly, or you can be unemployed."

Over the course of the season, Hopper learned a lot about getting along with people of other races. At the team's victory party, he approached Jackie. "You're a fine gentleman and the greatest competitor I've ever seen," said Hopper. "It's been wonderful having you on my team."

Jackie Robinson and Clay Hopper shake hands. Though Hopper didn't want a black man on his team, by the end of the season he had great respect for Robinson.

Robinson looks out over the playing field from the Royals' dugout. He led the team to the minor league championship in 1946.

LEADING UP TO THE MAJORS

All the while, Branch Rickey was preparing for Jackie's move to the majors. But there was still one thing that worried him. Rickey thought that if blacks cheered Jackie too wildly some **bigoted** whites might start fights.

As a result, Rickey started what became known as the "Don't Spoil Jackie's Chances" campaign. He urged blacks not to cheer too loudly or do anything that might **provoke** people who wanted to see Jackie fail.

Leo Durocher was a star shortstop before becoming the manager of the Brooklyn Dodgers. He was elected to the Baseball Hall of Fame in 1994.

In the spring of 1947, Rickey also tried to get the support of the Brooklyn team. He hoped that when the Major League players saw how good Jackie was, they would happily welcome him. After all, one great player could take a team all the way to the World Series. To showcase Jackie's talents, Rickey scheduled seven Montreal-Brooklyn practice games. Jackie lived up to his billing. He batted .625 and stole seven bases.

Jackie clearly had talent. Some Dodger players, however, still did not want Jackie to play in the majors. A few players signed a petition stating that they refused to play on the same team as Jackie. Rickey replied that anyone who wanted to quit was welcome to do it. Manager Leo Durocher was even more direct. "It doesn't matter to me whether the guy Robinson is blue or orange or black or if he is striped like a zebra. . . . I say he plays."

In the end, no Dodger player quit the team. Many even came to appreciate Jackie's talent and good character. On the morning of April 9, 1947, Rickey made the following announcement: "Brooklyn announces the purchase of the contract of Jack Roosevelt Robinson from Montreal." The Dodgers needed a first baseman. Jackie was their man.

Jackie Robinson holds up
his newly signed contract
with the Brooklyn Dodgers
on April 11, 1947.

ROOKIE OF THE YEAR

Less than one week later, Jackie became the first black
ballplayer to play in a Major League game. It was April
15, 1947. The Dodgers were playing the Boston Braves.
Brooklyn's stadium, Ebbets Field, was packed. Unfortu-
nately Jackie did not have a good game. He grounded out
to third base, flied out to left, and hit into a double play.

On April 13, 1947, just two days after joining the Dodgers, Robinson catches a ball at first base during an exhibition game against the Yankees.

The only time he reached base was on a defensive error by the other team.

Despite this, Jackie was making a sensation. When the Dodgers played the New York Giants a few days later, a crowd of 53,000 people came to watch. It seemed as though everyone was shouting, "Jackie! Jackie!" at the same time.

In that series, Jackie finally delivered. In four games he got five hits. He also slammed his first Major League home run.

Still, many players and fans refused to accept a black man in the Major Leagues. On April 22, the Dodgers played against the Philadelphia Phillies at Ebbets Field. The Phillies' manager, Ben Chapman, led several of his players in heaping abuse on Jackie. Every time Jackie stepped on the field they called him horrible names. Jackie called it one of the most unpleasant days of his life.

Jackie was tempted to march over to the Phillie dugout and start a fight. But he remembered his agreement with Branch Rickey. If he reacted violently, bigots would claim that a black man wasn't up to playing in the majors.

JACKIE'S GIFT

"To this day, I don't know how he withstood the things he did without lashing back. . . . Somehow . . . Jackie had the strength to suppress his instincts, to sacrifice his pride for his people's. It was an incredible act of selflessness that brought the races closer together than ever before and shaped the dreams of an entire generation."

—Hank Aaron, the Major League lifetime home-run leader

Even though Jackie couldn't respond, other Dodgers took up his cause. Eddie Stanky marched toward the Phillie dugout and cried, "Listen, you yellow-bellied cowards. Why don't you yell at somebody who can answer back?" Soon newspapers and radio shows were chiming in. They all were critical of Ben Chapman for his racist attitudes. Chapman later apologized. The next time the two teams played, he asked Jackie if he could have his picture taken with him. Jackie said yes, even though many Phillie players still taunted him from the dugout.

Luckily, Jackie's relationship with his own teammates got better and better. The Dodger shortstop was a man

The Brooklyn Dodgers congratulate Jackie Robinson on his home run during the second playoff game of the pennant race in 1951. Pee Wee Reese (wearing jersey number 1) was on base when Robinson homered, putting the Dodgers in the lead 2–0.

named Pee Wee Reese. At one game, fans asked Reese how he could stand to play with a black man. Without saying a word, Reese walked over to Jackie, put his arm on his shoulder, and began talking to him. Later Jackie said, "That meant so much. . . . It was just a kind and incredible gesture."

As the season went on, Jackie began to play up to his potential. Buses arrived in Brooklyn carrying people of all races to see the amazing man who had broken baseball's color line. By the end of the year, the Dodgers had the best record in the National League. Jackie hit .297 and led the league with twenty-nine stolen bases. He was named the National League Rookie of the Year. That fall the Dodgers played the New York Yankees in the World Series. Despite Jackie's seven hits, the Yankees won. But Brooklyn fans knew that one of the main reasons their team had gotten so far was Number 42: Jackie Robinson.

Jackie Robinson agreed to have his photo taken with Ben Chapmen only after the Phillies manager apologized for leading his team in making abusive remarks.

A HALL OF FAME CAREER

During the next ten seasons, Jackie was one of the best players in baseball. No one was more exciting. Fans knew they were in for something thrilling when Jackie got on base. He took large leads. He dared pitchers to throw to the base and get him out. He stole bases.

Jackie was also a fine hitter. Over his career, he collected 1,518 hits and retired with a lifetime batting average of .311. After playing first base during his first season, Jackie

Roy Campanella (right) and Jackie Robinson (left) stand with the Dodgers' new pitcher Don Newcombe at Chicago's Wrigley Field in May 1949.

switched to second base. He became one of the best fielders in the league. In 1949 he hit .342 and won the Most Valuable Player award.

With Jackie in the lineup, the Dodgers were always competitive. They won the National League championship six times. But the New York Yankees were also fielding some of their best teams ever. In 1947, 1949, 1952, and 1953, the Yankees beat Brooklyn in the World Series. In 1955, the Dodgers finally did it. They defeated the Yankees in seven games to win the World Series.

Though Jackie faced taunts and abuse throughout his career, over time most people grew to treat him with respect. To most Americans, Jackie was a hero. People of every race would stop to talk to him on the street. In 1950, a movie called *The Jackie Robinson Story* opened in New York.

Better still, other black players were soon playing in the majors. Don Newcombe became one of Brooklyn's best pitchers. Roy Campenella was one of the best catchers in the majors. When Willie Mays came up to play for the New York Giants in 1951, Jackie was there to give advice and offer encouragement.

To his credit, Jackie Robinson was never afraid to speak his mind. In 1949, many Americans feared that the country would be forced into a war with the Soviet Union. Some

"DID YOU SEE JACKIE ROBINSON HIT THAT BALL?"

When Jackie became famous there were a number of songs written about him, including "The Jackie Robinson Boogie" and "The Jackie Robinson Blues." One of the best known was "Did You See Jackie Robinson Hit That Ball?" It went like this:

> And when he swung his bat,
>
> The crowd went wild,
>
> Because he knocked that ball a solid mile.
>
> Yeah, boy, yes, yes. Jackie hit that ball.

Jackie Robinson speaks to members of the U.S. House of Representatives Un-American Activities Committee in July 1949. He shared his opinion that the majority of blacks in the United States would not consider spreading communism in their country.

leading black Americans felt that, after suffering through years of discrimination, black citizens shouldn't have to fight. Jackie was asked to give his opinion on the subject before Congress. Jackie said that he thought blacks should fight in a war if called upon.

In the early 1950s, several black churches in Miami, Florida, were bombed. At the time, the new Dodger general manager was Walter O'Malley. O'Malley said he did not want any of the Dodgers to comment on the bombings. Jackie disagreed. He spoke out forcefully against the bombings. He also spoke out in favor of **civil rights,** or the rights of all Americans to live and be treated equally. "I'm a human being," he said. "I have a right to fight back."

At age twenty-eight, Jackie had been older than the average **rookie.** By the time the Dodgers won the World Series in 1955, he was thirty-six and getting old for a ballplayer. After the 1956 season, Jackie's contract was sold to the New York Giants. But Jackie said that it would be unfair to the Giants to take their money. In his opinion, the Giants needed younger talent. Instead, Jackie retired.

Robinson waves a New York Giants pennant shortly after being traded to the team in 1956.

Rachel and Jackie Robinson relax at home with their three children.

LIFE AFTER BASEBALL

In the final years of his career, Jackie thought about his life after baseball. After hanging up his spikes, Jackie took a job as vice president for a coffee and restaurant chain called Chock Full O Nuts. He and Rachel lived with Jack Jr. and their two other children, Sharon and David, in a large house in Stamford, Connecticut. But Jackie didn't miss baseball. When Ebbets Field was knocked down to make way for an apartment complex, Jackie said, "I don't feel any loss."

* ★ ★ ★ ★

Perhaps Jackie didn't miss baseball because he was so busy. The 1960s were a time of great change. Black Americans began to speak out forcefully for their civil rights. As usual, Jackie was eager to get involved. He worked at the Harlem YMCA and became involved with organizations to

After retiring from baseball, Robinson became actively involved in the Civil Rights Movement. In February 1959, he spoke to the Federal Civil Rights Commission about equal housing rights for African Americans.

Robinson speaks to Rev.
Martin Luther King Jr. in
September 1962.

help blacks form successful businesses. He met with important civil rights leaders such as Martin Luther King Jr. and
Malcolm X. He always fought hard to help African Americans live in a country that treated them fairly.

* * * *

At the same time, Jackie was struggling with his health. Shortly after retiring from baseball he found out he had **diabetes,** a blood disease. Over time, the disease took its toll on Jackie. By the early 1970s, he could barely see. His heart was weak.

Tragically, in 1971 his oldest son, Jack Jr., died in a car accident. Still, Jackie Robinson continued to speak out for the things he believed. His last public appearance was at the 1972 All-Star Game. Jackie said in an interview that he would like the major leagues to have a black baseball manager. "I'd like to live to see the day when there is a black man coaching at third base."

LEADING THE WAY

The following is from a letter to Jackie Robinson that Senator John F. Kennedy wrote during his campaign for president in 1960.

I have long admired your contribution to the world of baseball and good American sportsmanship. Hearing your great personal concern about the denial of civil rights to American citizens by reason of their race or color. . . I believe I understand and appreciate your role in the continuing struggle to fulfill the American promise of equal opportunity for all.

Those days would come. Sadly, Jackie did not live to see them. On October 24, 1972, he died of a heart attack. Jackie was mourned around the country as a great ballplayer and an even greater man.

Jackie Robinson did what few people could. He played brilliant baseball under incredible pressure. At the same time he turned the other cheek to unspeakable abuse. In so doing he helped make America a fairer nation. Today, minorities have important positions in sports, business, and politics. We all owe a debt of gratitude to Jackie Robinson.

Glossary

bigoted—having strong, unreasonable beliefs, and insisting that other opinions are wrong

diabetes—a disease in which the body does not properly regulate the correct level of blood sugar

dignity—being honorable or worthy

inducted—admitted as a member

injustice—lack of fairness or justice

insubordination—disobeying authority

integrating—blending separate groups into a unified whole

prejudice—irrational dislike of a race or a group of
people

provoke—to annoy someone or make them angry

rookie—a new player

scout—someone who finds and contracts talented people

segregated—separated from others

superior—of higher rank or quality

Timeline: Jackie

1919		1936	1941	1942	1945	1946
Jackie Robinson is born in Cairo, Georgia, on January 31. That summer, Jackie's family moves to Pasadena, California.		Jackie attends high school in Pasadena, where he is a sports star.	Jackie becomes the first athlete in the history of UCLA to letter in four sports. He meets his future wife, Rachel.	Jackie joins the Army and serves until 1944.	Jackie plays for the Kansas City Monarchs in the Negro League.	Jackie and Rachel get married in Los Angeles. Jackie plays season with the Brooklyn Dodgers' minor league team, the Montreal Royals. He hits .349 and is the star of the team.

Robinson

1947	1949	1955	1957	1960	1962	1972

Jackie becomes the first African American to play in the Major Leagues. He is named National League Rookie of the Year.

Jackie wins the Major League Most Valuable Player award.

After years of trying, the Brooklyn Dodgers finally defeat the New York Yankees to win the World Series.

Jackie retires from baseball and takes a job as vice president of the restaurant chain Chock Full O' Nuts.

Jackie meets with Senator John F. Kennedy and discusses civil rights.

Jackie is inducted into the Baseball Hall of Fame.

Jackie dies on October 24 at the age of 53.

To Find Out More

BOOKS

Brashler, William. *The Story of Negro League Baseball.* New York: Ticknor & Fields Books for Young Readers, 1994.

Myers, Walter Dean. *The Journal of Biddy Owens: The Negro Leagues.* New York: Scholastic, 2001.

Robinson, Sharon. *Promises to Keep: How Jackie Robinson Changed America.* New York: Scholastic, 2004.

ONLINE SITES

The Library of Congress, American Memory—
Baseball and Jackie Robinson
http://lcweb2.loc.gov/ammem/collections/robinson/

Scholastic Internet Field Trip, Jackie Robinson
http://teacher.scholastic.com/fieldtrp/socstu/bleacher.htm

Index

Bold numbers indicate illustrations.

About the Author

Dan Elish is the author of numerous books for children, including *The Worldwide Dessert Contest* and *Born Too Short, The Confessions of an Eighth-Grade Basket Case*, which was picked as a 2003 Book for the Teen Age by the New York Public Library. He lives in New York City with his wife and daughter.